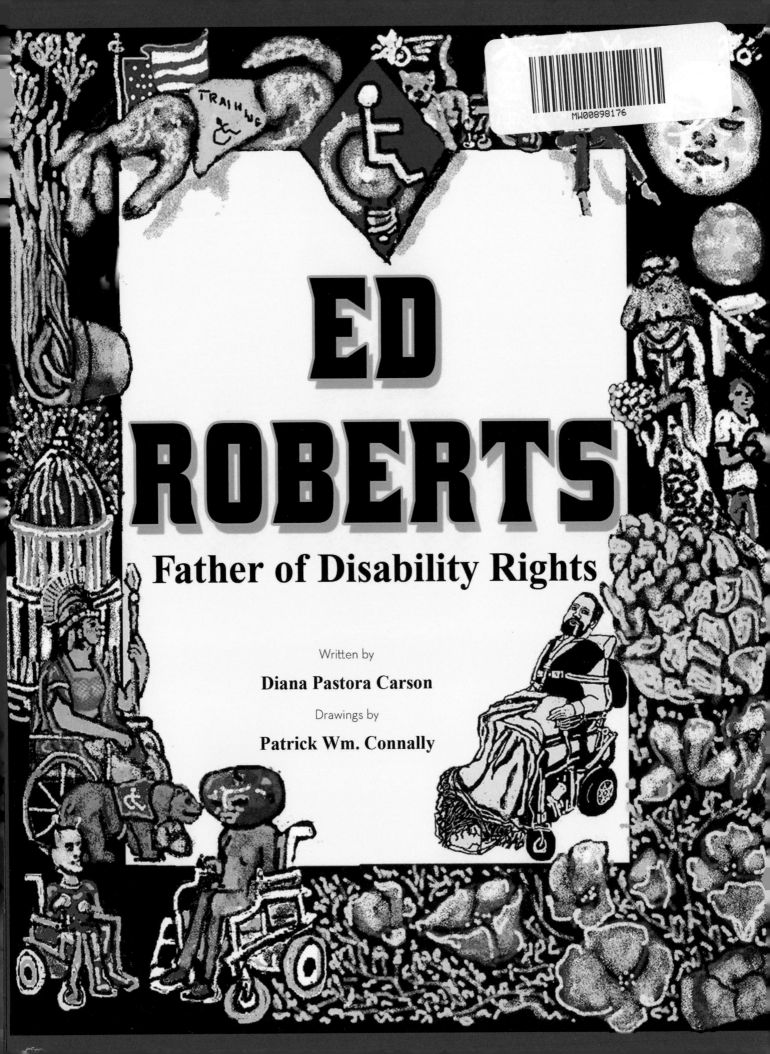

ED ROBERTS

Father of Disability Rights

Written by

Diana Pastora Carson

Drawings by

Patrick Wm. Connally

First published by Dog Ear Publishing
4010 W. 86th Street, Ste H
Indianapolis, IN 46268
www.dogearpublishing.net

ISBN: 978-1-4575-1952-9

This book is printed on acid-free paper.

Printed in the United States of America

Dedicated to all the heroes
of the Disability Rights Movement
and to those who continue to embrace
diversity and support life quality

"We have nothing to fear but fear itself"
Franklin Roosevelt
President with Disabilities

Ed Roberts was fourteen when it suddenly seemed that he would never go to college, get a job, or get married. Doctors made it seem that way. It wasn't because his family didn't have enough money or the right skin color. It wasn't because Ed had done anything wrong. It was simply because he now had a disability.

Ed Roberts hadn't always been disabled. From birth, he was an active boy. He could run before he was even a year old. He enjoyed organizing football and baseball games at the park across the street from his house. Ed was better in sports than anything else.

But in 1953, a virus called Polio took away his ability to walk, run, and play like he had before. Ed couldn't even breathe on his own. For eighteen hours a day, a device called an iron lung forced air into his lungs to help him breathe. Many people thought of Ed as a "vegetable" because of what he could no longer do.

Ed spent more than a year in hospitals before being able to go home. His iron lung went home with him. Since Ed could not return to school yet, he listened over the phone to his teacher while his peers sat in their classroom. Ed could move the toes on his left foot. So he used them to press a phone lever at the foot of the bed whenever he wanted to talk or ask a question. Ed knew that he needed an education now more than ever. His body had changed, but his brain had not. His education would help him to be whatever he wanted to be. So he worked hard and got good grades. By twelfth grade, Ed was able to return to school with the help of a wheelchair.

Ed learned that the hardest thing about being a person with a disability was overcoming unfair treatment by others. At the end of Ed's twelfth grade year, his principal was not going to let him graduate from high school. Physical Education and Driver's Education were required classes for a diploma. Ed hadn't taken those classes because the school didn't know how to include him. Ed learned lessons from his mother, Zona Roberts, as she fought the principal's decision. She would not give up until her son got the diploma he had earned. The principal finally gave in, and Ed graduated from high school.

When it was time for college, Ed needed help paying the tuition. A government agency that usually helped people with disabilities refused to help Ed. They thought it would be a waste of money for Ed to go to college. They said his disability was too severe and that he would never be able to work anyway. They were wrong. Ed fought that decision. He won and got the help he needed to attend college.

Finding the right college was not easy. Ed wanted to study Political Science. But the college he wanted to go to had too many hills and stairs. Ed's wheelchair wouldn't be able to get around. And where would he live? His wheelchair wouldn't be able to get in and out of an apartment without difficulty. His iron lung, which weighed 800 pounds, was too big and heavy for a college dorm room anyway. Though not many colleges wanted students like Ed, he would not give up.

Ed applied to the University of California in Berkeley and was accepted. Even though Ed was not sick, the only accessible place he could live on campus was in the university's hospital. Although it wasn't the ideal college life he had hoped for, he decided it was better than not going to college at all.

14

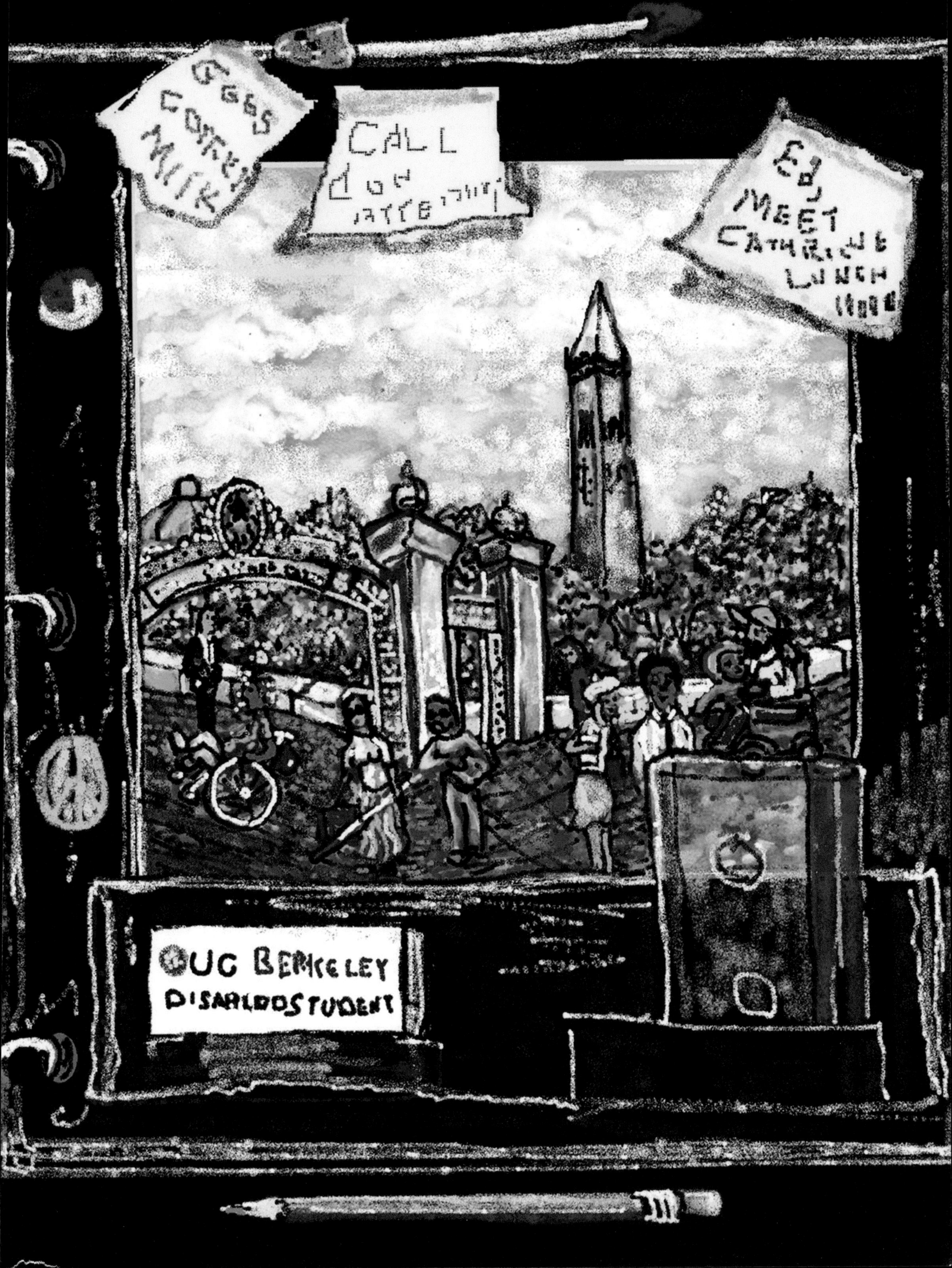
CALL
MEET
UC BERKELEY

Ed Roberts was the first person ever with significant disabilities to attend UC Berkeley. He needed help bathing, getting dressed, eating, and getting to classes. His brother, Ron, and friends, helped when they could. But Ed also hired assistants to help him with those things. Getting the help he needed made it possible for Ed to be successful in college. He made many new friends and inspired other people with disabilities to go to college.

Ed fit in perfectly at Berkeley. He loved learning about politics and the civil rights movements of African-Americans and women. Ed knew that he and others with disabilities were not suffering because of their disabilities. They were suffering because of discrimination, just like other minorities. Simply because they had disabilities, Ed and others like him were not treated with fairness and respect. While Dr. Martin Luther King, Jr. fought for equality for people of all colors, Ed Roberts fought for equality for people of all abilities. While Rosa Parks protested not being allowed to ride at the front of the bus, Ed Roberts protested not being able to ride the bus at all. Their fights were the same. They wanted equal opportunities. They wanted respect.

DATES + WORK
NO TO PITY
REAL HOMES NO Facilities
EDUCATION FOR ALL!
ADA
ACCESS IS A CIVIL Right!
FULL INCLUSION
LIBERTY TREE

Ed knew that people with disabilities didn't need others to feel sorry for them. They needed others to help them be more independent so nobody would feel sorry for them in the first place. They needed access to schools, houses, stores, and other buildings. They needed wheelchair ramps, curb cuts, bathrooms with wider stalls and handrails, money to pay assistants to help with daily activities, and public buses with wheelchair lifts. They also needed the same education and training as people without disabilities in order to have good jobs to be able to take care of themselves and their families.

After college in 1975, Ed was appointed by Jerry Brown, the governor of California, as the director of the Department of Rehabilitation. (This was the same agency that didn't want to *waste* money on Ed's college education because they didn't think he could ever work.) As the new director, Ed made many changes in California that helped people with all kinds of disabilities live more independent lives. Whether they had developmental disabilities, physical disabilities, learning disabilities, or mental health disabilities, he believed they could succeed. Ed believed that with the right access and support, anybody could achieve their goals. He was living proof.

Ed Roberts inspired people with all kinds of disabilities to stand up for their rights as well. In 1977, he and hundreds of others protested the government's lack of help for people with disabilities so that they could be more independent citizens. This protest was called the San Francisco Sit-Ins. Protestors with disabilities and their friends camped out at a government building, insisting that a law be enforced to grant equal rights and opportunities to people with disabilities. Many of the protestors risked their lives by staying, as they were often unable to receive necessary medical attention or food. But they and their allies continued strong and helped each other. After many weeks of protesting, Ed Roberts and his friends won the battle. Their courage and commitment had paid off. At a victory rally, Ed Roberts spoke these words:

"...We have begun to ensure a future for ourselves, and a future for the millions of young people with disabilities who I think will find a new world as they begin to grow up, who may not have to suffer the kinds of discrimination that we have suffered in our own lives, but that if they do suffer it, they'll be strong and they'll fight back. And that's the greatest example, that we, who are considered the weakest, the most helpless people in our society, are the strongest, and will not tolerate segregation, will not tolerate a society which sees us as less than whole people. But that we will together, with our friends, reshape the image that this society has of us..."

Later, through their continued fight, people with disabilities all over the United States began to enjoy the same benefits as non-disabled people. The Americans with Disabilities Act and other laws made sure that new buses are equipped with wheelchair lifts, sidewalks have curb cuts, public buildings have ramps, children and adults with disabilities attend the same schools as non-disabled students, and more money is used to help people with disabilities to be independent citizens throughout their lives. Ed wanted people all over the world to enjoy the same rights as Americans, so he co-founded the World Institute on Disability to help people in other countries as well.

Ed Roberts' courage and actions earned him many honors and awards. He traveled continuously, spreading the message of equality far and near. He met world leaders and shared his vision with them. He proved that people with disabilities can work and play together with everyone else. He made a difference for disabled people all over the world. Most importantly, Ed Roberts left this world a better place than it had been before.

Ed Roberts was born on January 23, 1939.

He died on March 14, 1995.

"They told me I'd be nothing but a vegetable.

Here I am an artichoke.

I choose to be an artichoke all prickly on the outside

with a big tender heart."

-Ed Roberts

Symbols are a way of passing on information through pictures. The illustrations in this book are rich with symbolism unique to Ed Roberts and the Disability Civil Rights Movement.

Page 3 - This combination dragon/rattlesnake has at least two meanings. In Chinese art and mythology, dragons are often seeking the "pearl of wisdom" or enlightenment. Dragons are symbols of power, strength, and good luck. This dragon has a rattlesnake tail. Rattlesnakes are symbolic of California, where Ed Roberts was born and raised. Snakes shed old skin and continue life in their new skin. They are also an early symbol of American freedom. "Don't tread on me" is a phrase that was often seen on flags with a snake symbol.

Page 9 – Frogs are symbols of transformation and enlightenment. They change from tadpole to frog in a short period of time. Ed's body changed. And so did his mindset. He learned many things through these changes. Ed learned to be strong, to believe in himself, and to fight to be a part of the community.

Page 11 - The Lucha Libre wrestler in the wheelchair represents the fighting spirit of Ed and his mother, Zona. The eagle with its wings spread symbolizes the American spirit and strength.

Page 13 - Dinosaur bones represent a system trapped in an old, outdated way of thinking. The scissors are for cutting through "red tape," or obstacles. Ants are symbols of how we can participate in our community: either as individuals, or by working together toward the same goals.

Page 17 - The jewelry is a symbol of the value of education. Ed cherished his education. It gave him power to achieve his goals. There are also two sign language letters on the page: a U on the left and an S on the right. Together they spell "us." We're all in this together.

Page 19 - The picture of Abraham Lincoln in a wheelchair represents how many people think of Ed Roberts. He was an important Civil Rights leader like Abraham Lincoln. He brought freedom, rights, and access to the American Dream into their lives. The knight represents the fight for a noble cause.

Page 23 - The boy at the bottom of the picture is Lee Roberts, Ed Roberts' son.

Page 25 - This is a modified Great Seal of California. In Roman mythology, Minerva is the Goddess of Wisdom and Civilization. The bear is a symbol of California, represented here as a service animal.

Page 27 - The man peeping over the top of the American Flag banner is a World War II symbol of solidarity among Allied Forces. It was accompanied with the phrase, "Kilroy was here." Troops had fun leaving this message for other soldiers so they would know that they were not alone. Ed Roberts wanted other people with disabilities to know that they were not alone in their fight for equality.

All Text Pages - The artichoke was Ed Roberts' personal symbol. He was told that he'd always be a "vegetable," (which, by the way, is a disrespectful thing to say). He decided that if people were going to think of him that way, he could at least have a choice in the matter. He chose to be an artichoke: "all prickly on the outside with a big, tender heart." Ed chose to love himself, disability and all, and to celebrate his life.

There are many other symbols in Ed Roberts: Father of Disability Rights. What do they represent? There are butterflies, wild flowers, a skunk, a star in a wheelchair, mazes, fireworks, a deer, a quail, planets, and many more symbolic illustrations. Can you figure out what they mean?

CPSIA information can be obtained
at www.ICGtesting.com
Printed in the USA
LVIC01n1339090114
368680LV00004B/27